for Nina

CSU Poetry Series LVIII

Short History of Pets

Carol Potter

Cleveland State University Poetry Center

ACKNOWLEDGMENTS

Grateful acknowledgment is given to the following journals in which these poems appeared for are scheduled for appearance:

Prairie Schooner: "Early Lessons in Electricity," "Short History of Love," "You Need A Girl With Teeth," "A Nice Piece with the Black Notes Missing"
The Massachusetts Review: "My Father, Dressed Like Trees," "The Housepainter Before Me," "Music She Insists," "Between A Poem and A Sentence," "The Limited Family Kitty"
The American Voice: "The Bright Bulbed Flowers," "Short History of Pets," "A Spoilt, Exquisite Air"
The Iowa Review: "And She Was Happy"
The Journal: "Three Crows," "Horse Tigers," "Salt-Wind off Truro," "Block Island Ferry"
Evergreen Chronicles: "Horse"
Field: "Nobody Drowned," "Four Days of Rain," "The Funk of Those Acres," "The Market," "Dead Baby and Gruff Daddy"
The Southern Poetry Review: "Waiting For Seven Birds To Fly in from Utica"

With gratitude for the Massachusetts Cultural Council for the Arts for financial assistance.

And to MacDowell Colony for the Arts, Centrum, Villa Montalvo, Yaddo, and the Fundacion Valparaiso where some of these poems were written.

Published by Cleveland State University Poetry Center
1983 East 24th Street
Cleveland, OH 44115-2440
ISBN: 1-880834-49-9

Library of Congress Catalog
Card Number: 00-104150

The Ohio Arts Council helped fund this program with state tax dollars to encourage economic growth, educational excellence and cultural enrichment for all Ohioans.

Short History of Pets

CONTENTS

I

II

III

IV

I

The real history of consciousness starts off with one's first lie...splitting the self off from the tribe, giving it air to breathe and freedom to breathe in....

Joseph Brodsky

NOBODY DROWNED

It's the green river of a childhood
in which nobody drowned.
No legs were broken.
None were shot though once
the shotgun went off in the house
three inches from the brother's head.
Someone's father hung himself in a red barn.
Sucking her thumb in third grade,
one girl pulled her hair out by the roots;
she was bald at the crown,
but nobody drowned.
A drunk father wearing ice skates
driving a tractor was hauling
a wagonload of children behind him.
There was one divorced mother
who smoked and had three names.
Teacher smacked a boy's head
against the wall.
Six cows were hit by lightening,
one run over by a truck,
three killed by dogs.
Two trucks turned over, a tractor
rolled down hill, crashed
into the woods,
but nobody drowned.
The brothers and sisters
chopped the heads off chickens,
hung frogs on wire fences.

They leaped from second floor
windows, practicing how to fall.
Sometimes the father pounded them.
Sometimes they pounded each other,
but nobody drowned.
One boy stuck another boy's foot
to the floor of a silage wagon
with a pitchfork, and the girls
rode their horses
into the river. Hands buried
in manes, pressed against
wet flanks, they floated
in the green river
bank to bank, and nobody
drowned.

You Need A Girl With Teeth

Sister needed to make sure her little friends
were tough enough. Some kind of Joan of Arc
at her side.   She took them one by one

and ran them fast through the fields to see
if they could keep up. Sometimes you need an army
next to you. Don't nobody be gasping for air.

Sister teaching her friend to stand
on the back of the horses. The friend falling,
and breaking her arm. Rode two miles home

with a broken arm.
All summer long the two of them
pretending to be Elvis Presley,

hair slicked into pompadours
Sister made a pretty good
Elvis. Better than brother downstairs singing

you ain't nothing but a hound-dog. Everywhere he went
that summer, that's what he sang.
When sister found breasts growing

on her chest, she sat in the bathtub
and wept.
Didn't want it.

Wanted to wipe them out.
Sometimes you need an army.
You need a girl with teeth.

Short History of Pets

Girl had a dog that bit people.
Bit the bread lady and the girl
from up the street. Bit the gas man.
Girl came home one day
and the dog was gone.
Asked mother and father
where the dog went.
They told her they took the dog
to the vet and the vet found
a new home for the dog.
The girl missed the dog but thought
of the dog in her new yard, some new
children. Girl knew the dog
was dead. Saw you could believe
two things at once.
Dog is alive. Dog is dead.
Mother and father sleep
in their bed, and daughter sits up
thinking of the dog happy
in her new home.
She sees how important the story
she tells herself is.
It's a good story.
Girl remembers the dog's
pink tongue. Thinks of that tongue
licking a new palm
in a new home. Dog under the table
eating what the new kids

won't eat. It's an easy thing.
You take a bite of food,
then wipe your mouth
with your napkin.
You stick the food in the napkin.
Then put your hand
in your lap, politely.
Open the napkin for the dog.
Let the dog eat what gags you.

MUSIC, SHE INSISTS

It was the horrible wonderful.
Bad good and the good cruel,
the real kind of harsh. Nothing indifferent.
You could be fodder. You could be
fuel, and the dark, magic fields singing,
all the time, singing.
Something for everyone.
A myth at each stanchion. Every door.
Each fly with a story at its lips and a belt at the waist.
The beautiful awful wonderful
grimace on mother's face
because sister was in the egg laden
dark cellar smoking cigarettes.
She was supposed to be doing something else.
Not singing those raspy folk songs.
It's music, she insisted. *I tell you:*
music. Father's supper was getting dry
because he was late from the field.
He was out in the dark plowing dirt.
There were seeds to sow, a harvest
to reap. All the family in the house
tuned to the sound of one wheel
spinning over the field perhaps,
and a man stuck beneath it.
Listening for the sound
of maybe nobody coming home
perhaps. Which is a large sound.
Something ringing in your ear.

Somebody banging an empty field with a pot.
They didn't want it any other way.
Didn't want to be the kid up the street
dressed like the Lone Ranger
in that goofy outfit with the fringe.
Didn't want to be the Lone Ranger.
It was the life they loved,
ducking when father came for them.
Tractor they forgot to set the brake on.
Sister letting the gleaming eggs she was supposed to candle
drop from her hands testing to see
which fell first, the feather
or the egg. A child at the corner
of the barn with a lie on each red lip.
There's a story here and everybody's talking.
You can smell it in the dark.
Egg yolk on the floor,
and the feathers sticking to it.
Children playing house everywhere.

DEAD BABY AND GRUFF DADDY

If the family builds itself
around the dead baby,
then everybody wants to be
the dead baby.
All ten children turn blue
in the face. Everybody
climbs into the crib
and acts like the dead baby.
It's not as easy as anyone might think
to hold your breath like that,
but it's a good baby.
Such a quiet baby.
Mother rocks the dead baby,
carries it on her breast.
Daddy's got the dead baby
on his shoulder.
It's the baby you don't forget
when you get off the train.
You don't leave it by the side of the road.
Or let's say you had the house
with the gruff Daddy everyone's scared of.
Board by board the boards of the house
try to be Gruff Daddy. The window panes
try to be Gruff Daddy.
The children pound each other
while Mother whispers into her soup
because Gruff Daddy's coming home.

Sometimes he takes his belt off
for the girls, rubber hose for the boys.
It's like anywhere you might live.
It could be Happy Mommy or Cracked-Up
Sister or simply Sick Brother
standing in the kitchen singing all day long.
There's always someone in a household
nobody wants to spill.
Clumsy as you are.

BECOMING UNRELIABLE

You can stop sorting the eggs.
Don't have to be the egg lady, the farmer's wife.
The farmer's daughter.
There's the basket of eggs.
Each one ripe with a new chicken.
A barn full of chickens,
beaks of chickens, the little nails
at the end of each talon.
Somebody gets the pecking.
The scabby one, the partly blooded bald one.
Layers of chicken shit on the floor.
The hunger of a barn full of chickens.
The pluck cluck of it all.
Wings opening, shutting in dust,
flutter between roost and chicken coop floor.
Guard the nest of eggs.
Here comes the egg girl to gather the eggs.
The egg mother drives the egg route
after the egg girl cleans the eggs
and sorts them. Small, medium, large.
Somebody has to do it.
It's the egg business.
There's feathers stuck to everybody.
You learn about duty.
How to do what you're told.
How to get free of it—that's the next study.
How to spot them—
eggs with blood on the yolk.

Eggs without.

There's a certain lightness to them.

You hold them in your hands.

Balance them on top of your head.

Swallow them whole.

Blow the yolk out and whip the white.

Drop them without breaking.

There's that smell on you though

long after the chickens are gone.

Egg shells sticking to your shoes.

You count to twelve.

Then you start again.

It's the counting syndrome.

There's an egg in your hand

and you're giving it a number.

AND SHE WAS HAPPY

Sister has learned how to walk around dry eyed.
She's picked up the knack.
Here she comes across the field
on a swollen ankle. Sprained it
running too fast around a corner.
She goes down to the stream,
puts the ankle in the cold water.
She can hear the cows in the barn—
their wet voices rolling downhill
to pool in the trees around her; water
with its tongue at her ankle, that chilled
bone, and she's happy listening
to the spring breeze in some slightly
budded trees, enough green in them
to keep them from clicking.
She keeps her eyes open
and her mouth shut. She's all
business. When the horse
threw her onto the road, knocked her
out, she woke up, saw the horse's
broad belly above her and she was
happy.   Horse could have galloped
home, but stayed. She stood up,
looked into the horse's eyes,
saw herself upside down
and out of shape.
Certain she saw remorse
in the horse's brown eye,

she was happy, and the world
she thought was full of mercy.
She got up on the horse
and rode home. Told no one
about her cracked head, the blood
on her shirt, where so much
happiness came from.

A Nice Piece With The Black Notes Missing

Sister was a bad guest sometimes.
Awake at 3 a.m. in someone else's house
and everybody sleeping.
It's not your refrigerator. Not your house you walk
in the dark. She broke things by mistake.
She is too big sometimes for where she is.
Like that time the parents were gone.
There was a big storm coming.
The children had put honey and peas in the cuckoo clock,
taken the keys off the piano.
They looked out the window, saw the black funnel
coming down the street.
Sister was on the wrong side of the locked door
so brother took her by the hands and hauled her under.
She came out flat as paper but smiling.
When the parents got home
the children prayed Mom and Dad
wouldn't notice the peas
stuck on the clock and 12 noon broken.
Brother sat at the piano, played
a nice piece with the black notes missing.

SHORT HISTORY OF A GIRL THIEF

Room for the roof of the world.
The stretch and reach of it. Trees, big patch of sand
and the ocean besides. Room for what you want.
And a girl's bright face. The place she stole from.
The jacket had large pockets. Room for a record, a book,
some pens. Something to smoke.
Room for the roof the world's pitch provides.
Loose shingles at the crown.
Room for a mistake. Roof ridge vast.
There's the expanse and the light rain
falling into it. The big bridge across the river
and the tremendous drop from the top.
We want to be able to recognize the mistake.
The slip of the foot is good.
The assurance of gravity and the long fall
off a high point. Want something that announces
itself. Store detective on each arm:
Stop right there. Come with us.
You're cocked between them like any criminal.
Clever won't do it this time.
Go ahead, there's room for tears and a lie or two.
It's a big world
and you can take a walk that won't finish.

CHILDHOOD THE REHEARSAL

You learn how to set the table.
How to pretend you ate what you didn't,
and the fields prepare you for silence.
For the furrows and the food that stands there.
For the harvest.
The great trucks full of silage coming toward you.
For what weighs and what has no weight.
Prepares you to identify the noise.
The tick of light on the roof of the house.
Handprints on door jambs.
The great fields and the river there.
To fix what was broken.
White blossoms in the pear tree and you
in the top of the tree as the wind blows through.
Sunlight in the blossoms blowing and your body opening into it.
The limbs rocking and you singing in the empty field.
You welcome the distance between house and forest.
Welcome the forest with no one in it.
The weight of cow and the sting of barbed wire
around the baled fields.
The heft of bales, and the body's rapture.
The dark at the roots of the grass.
In the rows of corn.
Where you children played house,
smoked pipes. Practiced kissing.
You could call this nostalgia.
The lit house of childhood
and the children running in the dark fields all around it.

II

Poor little beggar.
A human, if ever we saw one.

—Wislawa Szymborska

THE BRIGHT BULBED FLOWERS

Flee the house. Sell the piano.
Sell the oak hutch, and the child's
red wagon. A woman asks me if I regretted
having children at 19, at 24.
The firstborn daughter asking
if I could put the second one
back in my belly. The second one
screaming like a bald red bird
in my lap. As if you could
swallow it back in.
Like eating words.
I would like to say I regret nothing.
Even what I broke
and had no right to.
Not the marriage, nor the woman
I should never have left,
the woman on the motorcycle
headed for California.
The seat I did not climb up on.
The waist I did not put my arms around.
Regret with its thick stem
and its scarlet flower like a heart
at the end. What can you do with it?
Plant it. Pot it. Smoke it.
What good does it do?
Tell yourself it was a lesson
you needed to learn.

Edith Piaf singing,
je ne regret rien
and I don't buy it
though the voice is pure.
It's what I hope for.
Regret nothing. Wear it
like some kind of garland.
Something I could drape
around my neck, my arms.
The bright bulbed flowers
nodding as I move.

THREE CROWS

How the falling snow erases sound from the air.
It pleases me that the slur of cars on 47 is gone.
That I can hear no squirrels running in the dry leaves.
And the tree frogs, crickets that sang all summer
this is it, not much time, not much time they sang, are gone.
We subtract the color green, take away leaf from tree
and add the bare backs of hills that the leaves hid.
The ground has become stone and the small pond sheeted over.
What was alive in the water has buried itself in the mud.
Is dead. Does not bat itself against the bottom of the ice.
Does not stare at the sky through that shut door.
You can knock on the ground and nothing comes out.
Take away the voices summer plaits inside the green.
That profusion of leaf, each blade singing and the air
thick with sound. If grief comes walking now, you can see it.
Something dark, and glossy in the bare field. Three crows.
Voices clear and gratified by their own clarity. It is too late
to paint the house before winter comes, to finish raking leaves.
It is winter. Let the snow fall. Let it freeze and the roads get slick,
the wind drag itself house to house fingering what needs to be taken.
What needs to be blown before it. The dead branches off the trees,
and the leaves that didn't fall but hang like paper rattling.
Let the wind take them down. Scrub the trees and cover the ground
around this house. Let it be done. Let it be over with. Take away
what needs to be taken. Let it be taken. Even the beagle all day
on the neighbor's stoop crying *oh, oh, oh,* has gone inside.
Sleeps in front of the fire, the great pink tongue retracted.

GREEN DOME IN A CLEAR SKY

Two draft horses on the top of the green hill hold the hill in place.
Massive bodies, metal shoes.
The great weight-bearing bulk of the both of them
standing on a green dome against a clear sky.
This is the known world and they've got it pinned.
Grass coming in green is not a bell banging
beneath them. Smell of dirt being dislodged
as the grass grows is not a grave being dug.
The green field is not a house with nobody in it.
Leaves open on distant trees;
fine green dust of pollen in the air.
Dust is dust. Is not ashes.
The grass is grass. Is not a highway.
Is not a woman in a car driving past
wondering where her children went,
but glad to have them gone
and guilty in her gladness. In her grief.
The hill is a hill. Is not a grave.

SOMETHING LADYLIKE

There's no truce, ever, with the furies—Carole Maso

She's standing in the phone booth
striking the hand set into its cradle

because she can't get through.
No one sees her banging.

It's a good thing.
It's something you could be arrested for.

She has a history of it.
Her brothers laughing and her

trying to kill them.
Wanting to fly through the air,

sink her teeth into them, one, two, three.
It was something to see.

Her red face and her teeth clacking.
They were something she could smack

with impunity. Brother bending over
his punched in gut. Right hook

to the solar plexus, but nobody told
because she was a girl

and it was embarrassing to get hurt by the girl.
Nothing you would admit to.

She did it on the piano.
Sometimes the wrong notes

made her mad and she'd bang the keys
with her fists. Nobody seemed

to mind. Smashed her hand
through the living room window.

Saw you could get away with it.
Break something and nobody know.

Lie about it and get away with the lie.
Then she grew up and had the baby.

The roaches ran from the stove;
the husband read the paper.

The baby cried. She took the carving knife,
lifted it over her head, jammed it into

the cutting board. You can still see it,
the end of the knife bent over though the husband

long gone and the children grown.
Something ladylike because nobody saw.

It's the other side of heartbreak.
Mother in the kitchen with the kids

and the kids not noticing
the thing happening but it's happening.

There's a hole in the kitchen and the air going out.
The kids are at the table eating their macaroni and cheese.

There's the sweet smell of vodka but nobody's drunk.
Nothing's on fire. It could look like anywhere.

The yellow mouths of the children.
Fake cheese on their lips like face paint.

The Body

It bleeds or it doesn't. Heats up,
sweats when it wants. Gets cold.
Wakes at 4:30 to hear the birds sing
and think about things
it can't do anything about.
Likes to turn itself over and over.
Takes a walk when it wants.
Breaks its own back. Sits in a chair
you'd never dream of sitting in.
Skin has marks on it because
it couldn't stretch wide enough for the business
and now the business is done—
the child grown and gone.
You could search all night
with your flashlight around the edge
of the pond if you want
try to find her lying out with that boy
you never suspected she was even seeing said
she was just going out for a minute
to look at the stars.

THE LIMITED FAMILY KITTY

*You'd better know the story and you'd better know
the child before you put them together–* Jane Yolen

Let's say it was the wrong story but the correct child. The limited family kitty.
Wrong child. Correct story. It's time for your shots now. Right needle.

Incorrect child. Proper remedy. Let's say good crows were out in a bad field
but the child got the story wrong. Had a funny way of mixing facts.

Her parents were not the Christian Fundamentalists. Daddy was not in the militia.
Brother had never been to jail. It was the right story but it wasn't hers.

She was on her knees every night but it still happened. Wrong daughter.
Right mother. Bad sister. Crazy father. It's the Hansel Gretel Story.

The little children with the bread crumbs everywhere you turn.
Somebody's going back to the orphanage even though she won the spelling bee.

She shows you the trophy. It's the correct world but the wrong door.
The bassinets mixed up maybe. Wrong tags on their wrists. Footprints

to the right town but the wrong boy. There's that story on your lips again.
Right kind of sky. But what child is it walking up to the horse? She's dropping

apples as she walks. Birds peck at the apples. The horse comes to her willingly.
She climbs through the fence. She drapes her arms over the horse's neck.

It's not her horse. Not her field. The woman leaning in the doorway of the barn
wants to comb out her hair. There's horse nettles in it. She'll get sent back

to the orphanage. Who told what to whom? Whose story is it? It's the wrong story.
There's that lie on the lips and the king with his pants pulled down.

No such thing you want to say. The orphans are walking past the gate.
Can't believe their good fortune to be in the same city as the great men

and the famous monuments. The famous house. The mothers are sending
the children back. Who can afford to keep them? The orphan is knitting herself

a little blanket. She's got the needles clicking. The stitches are a bit stretched out,
but she's okay with it. Back you go. Maybe it's the mother takes a lover story

and the kids outside the door can't help but listen to the love cries.
Everywhere they go they make that sound and no one can figure them out.

And who is that behind the door with Mom? The little lost children story.
The one with the bread crumbs and the pig's heart.

They ate the heart and were suckled by the grieving wolf. Mommy's new lover
wants to comb out your hair. Sister is singing to the swans. Father's taking

the children into the forest. The girl has gone up the beanstalk. Mommy's in trouble
down at the welfare. She's leaning over the man asking him if he wants her blood.

She pretends to slash her arm in his face. He falls back when she leans over him.
There they are the little kids jumping up and down in the sunlight

singing: *Take me. Take me. Take me.* That little jump rope game they like to play.
It's alright now. It's a short story. This won't take long.

EARLY LESSONS IN ELECTRICITY

Two feet of snow at the door, and the power gone three days.
Trees toppling; electric wires live on the ground.
In the light of one candle, I am brushing my hair.
Sparks lift as I brush. I am comforted
by the soft light, by the sparks from the brush.
How in the absence of sound, any one sound
becomes distinct. The crackle of hair, flame at the end
of the wick. I make my hair stand on end. It snaps
in the candlelight, and I remember early lessons
in electricity. Mary and I playing with our hair in the dark.
Making it spark. Mary and I touching the electric fence.
Practicing how to take it and not squeal.
Mary in the summer field taking the ends off fireflies,
then sticking them to her lids. Mary walking through
the dark field with her eyelids glowing.

MERINGUE

It was not the white meringues
on the cookie sheet in a dark kitchen

nor the woman who offered her
meringues. It was not the taste of the warm

meringue in her mouth. Nor the porcelain
dolls the woman kept in a trunk upstairs.

It was not the root cellar in the hill outside
the kitchen, nor the door that opened into the hill.

It was not the vegetables in the dark earth
nor the sun setting off the windows

so red one evening the girl thought the house was on fire
and the porcelain dolls, the meringues—fuel.

There was no fire. There were daffodils in formal gardens
and pathways of stone steps between terraces.

A red rose filled the sun room.
Red petal in each corner it seemed. Redder

than the heart in her chest
she thought. It was not the red rose

nor the egg man who was half-man, half-
woman nor the solidity of cows

in the field, the stand of pines around the pond
nor the cool dark heart of the pond she dove into.

What I know About Mercury

The ocean looks like mercury today. It gives and it takes away.
I'm paddling and the wave lifts me, pushes me forward, makes me think
I've moved but I'm still at the same people on the shore— pink and white

umbrella. Yellow dog. It's a slow progress forward but moving all the time.
Oil like dark of deep, gray sheen on top of it, metallic. Mercury.
The teacher who taught us about mercury killed himself the summer

after he had us. I can see him staring at a drop cupped in a glass dish in his palm.
Come look at this, he said, *how the metal breaks and gathers and breaks again.*
What it does when it falls on the floor. It was eighth grade. President Kennedy

had not yet been killed. None of us in that class had gone to Vietnam
and not come back; nobody pregnant, none of us gone broke. Last night I stood
at a pay phone next to the bay talking to my lover who told me not to come back she's

pulling the curtain, she's done with all this coming and going, these questions
about love. Waves were smacking the breakwater. *Can't hear you,* I kept saying.
It's the ocean. I held the receiver up to the night so she could hear the waves,

the wind, the black phone crusted with salt. That teacher who killed himself
did it in his mother's apartment. No one told us exactly how. The grown world
did what it had to do without us. We didn't ask.

IT'S GONNA BE REAL GOOD BABY

I didn't know it was a house of detention—
for some reason boys contained shouting from the upper windows
as I walked up the street two days stupid listening to the wind
stroke the corner of the building and make the sound of mouth
over empty bottle, until today, curious, I went to stare at the statue
at the foot of the building: man, woman, two children in concrete,
10 feet high, and flood- lit behind which a homeless man was making
up his bed. Boys were shouting out mesh-covered windows
to three girls in the grass.   Makeup and high heels,
teenagers in shoes that wobble. *Get Jimmy!* the girl yelled up at the window.
Then Jimmy shouting down to her something about what he's going to do
when he gets out next week, *It's gonna be real good baby.*
There's a circle of moon in a blue-black sky above the sycamores,
bare and patched with their own bark,
and the sky the color of something it hurts to want.
The man making his bed pulled the blankets up to his chin
undisturbed by the boys shouting and the girls standing in the grass
calling up to them. This almost sweet sound from detention.
The boys inside and the bright lips of the girls with their faces
turned up to the windows, moon ticking through the branches.
The lighting, random. The music, reckless.

FOUR DAYS OF RAIN

Face of a girl taped up around town.
I open the door of the 7-11,
pull her toward me, then let her
drop. Gone like the towns
beneath the reservoir. Streets,
places erased. A man in front of me
is buying scratch tickets. Can't decide
between Black Jack and Lucky Ride.
Scratch them someplace no one can see.
Throw the ticket out the window.
Rub the next one. Watch the number come up
from beneath your finger.
What you were hoping to see
stares back at you, or doesn't.
You see them alongside the road,
windows already scratched out,
paper bent in two.
Think you could follow them
back to the person's house.
Some people imagine the flooded towns
lifting out of the reservoir.
That you can see one of the steeples
when the season is dry.
Water goes to Boston
and they drink from us.
Four years ago, my friend's ashes
in the water, chips
flashing at us at they sank.

I drive home past the Mickey Mouse
with the windmill belly.
Past the plaster ducks, the Virgin
in half a tub, and the pair
of giant red heart balloons
on the front porch of the gift shop
across from the fruit stand
where my check bounced.
Hearts in the window
big as buoys, as if the heart
was a bladder you could inflate at will.
If this rain went on raining.
If this reservoir spilled.

LET THE DEAD

Today in the museum, I stared at the skeleton
in the glass case. Pre-Columbian, cupped around
itself, ribs arced, fingers almost touching its lips.
The ribs reminded me of the ribs of a boat.
The backbone, the keel. I imagined
strapping canvas to those bones, sticking a mast
in the spine. You'd have to unhook the fingers
from the lips. A little puff of wind.
Let the dead take you where they will.

YOUR IMPETUOUS FOOT

When you're a kid getting hit across the room
it's something like having an automobile accident.
You're never quite sure where you'll land.
But you know where you are because the voices

in the room are familiar. Someone crying out,
Oh No! but not stopping the accident.
Mom. Dad. Or maybe big brother's gone off,
and you're it. There's that accident over and over.

When something tips between two trees
it stays tipped.
You can hardly forgive the road.
The bald tires, your impetuous foot on the pedal.

You get out of the truck and think you can
put it back up on its wheels again.
You even try it once. Try to lift it up off its side.
There's the dust flying out of the compartment.

Your friend somewhere inside.
The metal of the truck bent, the axle bisected.
And that stupid station you were listening to
when you put your foot on the gas.

BLOCK ISLAND FERRY

Three decks packed with people trying to see
red sun going down, and a woman below going mad.
We can hear the woman screaming over the engines
and the sound the sea makes with the wind.
A man is brushing his long hair, drinking from a bottle
inside a paper bag, stretch pant cinched at the waist so his balls show.
Beside him, two women kiss, and another woman
stares at all three of them sideways. We are all of us
full of sunshine, a day at the beach, and the woman
howling from down below is howling closer, coming
toward us up the stairs in the arms of a young man grimacing.
She is too much for him, pitching and wailing in his arms,
stiff like a child kicking she arches her back at the top
of the stairs, threatens to launch herself from the rail,
but he's got her good. Cursing all the way to the captain's cabin,
she parts the people packed cheek to cheek trying to get a good view of her.
Some laugh when she passes; some can't get enough of it;
some don't know what to do. *Rape*, she screams from the cabin,
Rape! We can hear her thumping inside the pilot's house
like a large bird mistaking glass for sky.
She's kicking him, she's butting him with her head;
she is trying to get at the captain but the young man has her tight.
There's a certain glee on deck, with a punch in it.
That spanking some want to give her, something dirty
with a giggle. Pull her pants down, smack her good.
Fuck you, she yells, *Fuck you*. The drunk standing next to me
knows what he'd do with her. *Throw the bitch overboard,*

his wife says, and they laugh because it's like some sort of holiday
on board, everybody glad she's nobody's daughter, she's not my
lover though I stood next to her on the way over—
that whole long sunny gorgeous day ahead of us.
She was so quiet looking over at the island,
so quiet staring down at the sea.

THE REST IS TRAGIC HISTORY, HE WROTE

You've got to be careful about what you feed. The children bulking up
at the table. The one with the bald crown. After supper, he's down
at the corner chanting and sister's getting dressed up in camouflage.
She's in the back room oiling up her guns. *There's an answer*, she says,
 to everything and by gum I got it. Scratch it and the story starts to talk.
There is the inevitable smell of it. Gunpowder. Chalk from the classroom.
A lost mother's lipstick print on the glass. One of the kids
in the liquor cabinet, and the rest of them out back around the fire.
They're burning the family trash and there's a special smell to it.
Homework. Glue. Last night's liver. It's not necessarily a sad story.
There's something normal about it all. Even the head of the militia
is on a diet. She's watching her weight. Gun belt cinched at the waist
and the breasts accentuated. There's something sexy about almost anything.
And you're thinking maybe we should just go on being strangers.
You could be content staring from the car as you drive past.
A little wave maybe, a nod. Not so bad you think. Here's the story
and who wants to hear it? Out back in the country Mom and Dad
discover the camouflage. There's a target and it's moving and you realize
maybe it's you. When you walk by Sister's room you try not to imagine her
sighting at your chest but your nipples itch each time you pass that door.
You think of that muzzle with its little black eye watching you.
And second sister in bed all day. The one that picks at her face;
when she gets up you can't get her to stop talking. She says something odd.
The alter personality perhaps and we all sit there pretending we don't hear.
There's a little ring ring in my ear. Let me tell you about it.
The voices in the street below. Last night I thought it was a crazy person praying.
That little prayer that speech is, even the *fuck you* prayer, the *please go away*
prayer, *Listen to me, listen to me.* Everybody smile. There's a new day coming.
Sister's at the top of the stair, and she's singing.

THE MARKET

In the photo, the log the boy carries is three times
longer than he is. His short hair
makes his head round and smooth as a ball
in the center of the photo, log sticking out
equally on either side of him.
He is walking down the middle of a long, broad
street that's been bombed and strafed
and mortared, all the people gone
as if the world were a cup you could tip.
The log he carries touches the ruins
at each end it seems.
The boy's beige coat is cocked to the side,
bare back of one calf exposed to the camera.
Shoes with one sock.
Caption says *boy carries firewood to his home*
two miles away. On one side of the street,
bare rods of concrete houses poke into the air
like bones out of skin. One telephone pole
still standing leans to the left.
What to make of a world picked bare by adults?
Even the log he carries has been rubbed smooth.
We would understand if in the next photo,
boy was lying in the street
next to the log, caption simply stating
boy has had enough, like the ten year old
in Patzcuaro, 7 a.m., weeping on the cool pavement
next to his charcoal heater.
Every other day of the week he was unremarkable

because he sat, sold coffee,
went home. All the vendors were in place.
Piglets at the corner eating alfalfa,
tied to the phone pole.
Farmers bringing in milk for the morning,
pouring it container to container, tall aluminum cans
shining in the back of the trucks
while the boy on the pavement
sobbed, his shirt lifted from his belly
and the muscles twisting like a rope.
Mama, mama, mama, he was sobbing.
She was selling bread in the back
of the market, past the blankets,
the watches, the bananas.
None of the vendors could leave their stations
to take him to her,
and I could barely speak the language.
Somebody finally picked the boy up;
small enough to be carried easily,
he flailed electric in the man's arms
because whatever was hurting him
did not want to be touched.
I watched him
disappear into the market.
Could hear him above the heads of the crowd
until his voice was like the voice
of any one of the other vendors, the words
indistinguishable.

MY FATHER, DRESSED LIKE TREES

On the kitchen table, my father's
animal calls sit between the honey
and the porcelain cow butter dish.
There's one that sounds like mice
being devoured. Another one, a caught
rabbit. He says it is to bring
the larger animals towards him.
I don't know what it is like
to drop an animal, to see it fall
when you pull the trigger,
but every year there was a deer
hanging in our garage, hide
stripped off, head set up
on display. How red it is
inside an animal. How distinct
the smell of something opened up
from the inside out—that cavity.
Finally there is no more blood, nothing
dripping from the carcass.
We laugh with him when he demonstrates
the calls. Earlier, my father, my brother
and I sat in the kitchen listening
to my grandmother's message
on the answering machine.
Three times we played it back.
Jean don't cancel me out.
Don't cancel me out,
she said calling

from the nursing home.
She can't get what she wants,
but we aren't sure if what she wants
is to come north, or to stay
where she is. *Don't*
cancel me out, she said.
I think it's the only thing
we ever really want—
And what of my father
crouched in the woods,
dressed like trees, making
animal sounds, my father
sighting down the barrel of the gun
while something steps
through the trees
to greet him.
My father with his wild turkey call.
His broken rabbit call.
The sound of mice being eaten.

THE FUNK OF THOSE ACRES

What looks back at you from the woods.
From somewhere in the field.
It was not your province so you
couldn't flee. Impatient,
you wanted to shake the trees
and make them come out.
Wanted to snap the snow, make them
appear in their tracks.
What looks back from the hole
at the center of the tree.
What moves is edible if it were visible.
Bare palm of a mole
in the snow, mangled fur.
You held it in your glove, small nails
at the end of each finger. What moved.
What was found out, was a small red heart
running across snow, sweet meat in the mouth.
What's been here but isn't any longer.
Think if you stare long enough
at the landscape, something will step into the field.
Come to graze off the dead.
To eat the bittersweet draped tree to tree.
You are looking at them but can't see them;
they stand in the field and are the same color
as the field. As the trunks of trees.
As the breath from your mouth.
You think you will see them walk towards you.
Shake the stick in the snow,

and nothing moves. Clap. Shout.
Wave the grain bucket and whistle.
You walk through the field singing
and only you moving.
You like thinking about where they might be.
Imagine the funk of those acres.
Hair on the trees, on the wind.
The warmth of their bodies
melts small black patches beneath them.
They move when you move and they watch you.

III

I can't tell if the day is ending, or the world,
or if the secrets of secrets is within me again.

—Akhmatova

HORSE

I told you I felt angels fly from my body
when you were making love to me.
In love, in love, I told you.
Of course, the next day you and I fight.
How disappointed I am today
walking my heart up this steep hill
determined to turn it back in the right direction,
to take its mouth out of the dark trough
where it sometimes feeds.
Today this heart is like a horse
with a hard mouth; you can't stop it
no matter how far you lean back on the reins.
When I was a girl, someone showed me
a plant deadly to horses, two banks of green,
feathery fingers on Hinkle Road—
and the horse I couldn't control.
If she wanted to go back to the barn,
she went. When she needed to dump me,
she dumped me.
I sat on that horse uneasy.
It was her appetite I was afraid of.
Escaped one day, she broke into the grain barrel,
ate so much she made herself sick.
I had to keep her on her feet,
make her walk so her stomach wouldn't burst.
I was a ninety pound girl at the end
of a full-grown horse.
I pulled and pulled on the rope,
but she stood still, legs
locked, frozen like a giant bell.
Impossible to ring.

SALT-WIND OFF TRURO

Between us and the salt-wind
there is only this sliding glass door sheeted in salt.
The wind has definition this afternoon.
You can see the outline of it
forcing the bay hard against the beach,
whites waves smacking outside our door.
You came up out of our love making
weeping, and I kept thinking it was the wind
did it, unstuck your dead father from his keeping place.
How is it a dead man
can rise out of the arms of two women
making love? How is it you and I
could produce a death, your heart
in the salt-wind?
He was the age you are now when he died.
I was making love to you, you were
singing in my hands, and then
I saw the buildings of the Bronx
had built themselves on the shoreline
outside, saw the salt-wind
turning each window of those buildings white,
saw your face at each window
as they were carrying
your father out of the house.
I like to think we can keep grief
from each other
but what can any of us do
in the face of a street
with that many houses, a city
with so many streets?

SHORT HISTORY OF HEARTS

It's a problem with the heart because both parents have it.
Father's got leg veins where the heart veins

used to be, and Mother could drop dead at any time,
the heart in her chest a thin muscle, a glove with no hand

on bad days. Daughter would like to have a removable heart
like the heart of the Christ she saw in Mexico.

Everywhere she went they were outside his robe
like a pin he was wearing. A medal you could

take off. You could put it on. A perfect red heart,
perfect as the hearts of cows in the mercado,

and the small dogs dancing around those hearts.
How attentive the dogs were—

following the fingers of the butcher
as he moved through the carcass.

Every time he waved to his friends, they
leapt into the air, exultant.

THE PIANIST

If I had known these moths were coming in, I would have
shut the door long before dark. It is dark now, and the storm
that traced itself around the edge of the valley did not come.

All evening I listened to the wind blowing through my house,
and the tree making the sound of a door closing. Today,
when you were with me, it seemed you were somewhere else.

You told me when you were a girl, you lay down on the piano bench,
moved your hands up and down the keyboard to make your mother
think you were practicing. As long as sound was coming out,

she didn't care. The wind tonight is erratic, carries the sound
of the train two miles away, that whistle like a chorus of a thousand
throats wide open in the dark. A moth touches my skin, startles me.

Somehow we have to live with what we can not do for each other.
I know in your house in the next town, you can hear this same train
passing by. First your house, then mine.

WHATEVER WAS BROKEN

Down the hill, the sound of a hammer.
It is close to the end of summer.
What will soon fly off, or die
sings in the trees, in the grass.
One cricket stuck in the corner
next to my front door.
The hammer starts, stops, stops.
Whatever was broken has been fixed.
So much promise, one nail
pinning one board into place.
I will go about my business today
as if something was not coming
to an end. Already I can see myself
doing what I need to do not to miss you.

MIGRATION

It is the end of summer and I am willing myself
to be done with this grief.
It is like wanting to believe in God

because the absence is so large.
Light falls out of the day sideways.
No mistaking this for the end of summer.

It is the taste of it.   Wild grapes
ripening, warm in the sun—
skin of the grape slides down your throat.

If you stop. If you eat it.
And the almost mechanical
sound of crickets rasping all day

in blades of grass surrounding my house.
It is a sound you could lie down inside
like a tent. You could climb into it

and be gone. There is no
mistaking that cool breath
in the dark of the woods,

the stream already too cold to touch.
Birds putting their flocks together
alongside roads—synchronized flight,

balletic, this beautiful sky.
No clouds today.
Nothing to keep you here.

WAITING FOR SEVEN BIRDS TO FLY IN FROM UTICA

Such a view they have, pigeons lined up
along the girders of the bridge facing south,
beaks pointed into the sun.
They've got the Holyoke Range, they've got
the meadows, and the river gliding below them gleaming.
I stood last week with my brother outside his loft
waiting for seven birds to fly in from Utica.
Two were already in. He told me some get confused.
Fly off with birds from another flock.
I think of them watching the tail-feathers of the wrong bird.
Watching the tip of the wrong wing, following it back
to the wrong city, wrong loft.
My brother says they get tired.
If you work them too hard they don't come back.
There's a magnetic field in their brains,
a compass points them home.
He's eating his lunch on the deck of the loft.
He's got a sandwich, a jar of ice tea,
his youngest boy waiting with him.
He's watching the sky, wants me to see the birds
coming in but they don't.
I'm not sure which direction to look in.
Behind us, there's the barn,
his oldest boy in the milking parlor.
There's the blank sky over the trees.
Throw the pigeons in the air and they come back.
Put them in boxes and drive them 400 miles away,

and they come back.
Inside the loft there's the sound of that liquid
in pigeon's throats. The warble they make
with their beaks closed. There's the sound
of wings, birds rearranging themselves
one perch to another,
dust in the air when they fly up.
From the loft there's a view of the hills.
On the hill below the loft I once tried to kill
this same brother.
The loft wasn't there then.
There was no milking parlor just cows in stanchions.
There was snow on the hill,
and we were rolling down the hill
in each other's arms, swearing.
I had one ski on and the other one off.
I had just shoved his skis down the hill
because he did not want me to ski
over his ski jump he was so busy
patting, patting, making the lip
just so. There was his bare skull
and the ski at the end of my leg.
I was trying to swing it around and beam him.
I was hoping to kill him
as siblings sometimes hope with each other.
There was snow in my mouth.
Snow in my pants. Snow caked on his head.

We were pummeling and cursing
end over end, trying to teach each other
something neither of us wanted to learn about love.

Horse Tigers

It was a 43 mile drink of dark from your house to mine.
Stars, lights in houses and white shapes
of snow-lit hills, but a drink of dark at the end of which
in my house I lay down alone

to watch the great herds of zebras on TV,
rainfall determining where they will travel to next.
43 miles, and 45 minutes and then I watched
an entire pride of lions lounging in the cooling mud; zebras

off to the side waiting for their chance to drink, but the hippos
already into it, their great pink mouths yawning at the center
of the waterhole. It had been a long dry season.
One dead zebra at the edge of the hole, face down,

head under water and the vultures dancing on it, great wings
spread wide. It was 43 miles, me thinking
I'd made a fool of myself staring into your eyes
and finding myself stunned, without speech,

grinning, though we'd only just met. Your hands
on my face, how all of me wanted to just simply
lean into your touch completely—
the two of us trying this time to be smart,

we say, not impetuous, not stupid.
Not the same mistake over and over.
Staring and talking and the tentative touch
of hand on face, talking as if the words

in right sequence might be some kind of talisman
against disaster. I want to talk to you now about the light
gleaming on the black river as I crossed into Turners.
How satisfying the lattice-like shape of the long green bridge

bank to bank. Then the man with the reassuring
animal kingdom voice telling me *with the coming
of the rains, we see a new pattern emerge.* I sat
in my house watching the grasses grow in the rain

falling on the Serenghetti. Time-lapse photography.
Stallion mounting mare, then the foals suckling,
and the lions gone off on some other business.
It was a 43 mile drink of dark, watching for ice slicks

where sun had melted snow, ladled it across the inside
of curves to freeze in the dark. Even your cat was suspicious,
eyeing me all evening then finally, just once
lightly rubbing against my leg and leaving the room.

I Do What I'm Told

Write a poem with the word flesh you whispered
as I lay my body down on top of yours pressing
my mouth to that soft skin at the back of your neck
or was it my tongue at the base of your spine, fine hairs
lifting as I stroked ass to shoulder, sunlight in my face
and no sign of danger anywhere, the flesh of summer sky
in place, my nipples following the wet track of my tongue
traveling center to round of ass lifting beneath my weight
you rolling us over breasts to belly to mouth, *take me* you
whispered, though you're always wondering where
the hole in this boat might be, the broken oar
on the river, flesh of green leaves at the window
and the flesh of what happens when I can't touch you can't
take you into the field show you the green
flesh of rye grass full stem blowing seed, seed everywhere
and the green wind passing through wet of bird song at 4:30 a.m.
something so thick I could put my tongue on it. Waking today
without you I found the flesh of June air with its fine green dust
drifting off trees flowers open and pollen beading at the edge
of each lip as I walked into the flesh of sunlight
thinking of you yesterday morning telling me to write about
flesh of lupine, poppy, and the grass around the small
maples sunlight on your face as I entered wet sweet
at the center of you no longer whispering to me about the poem I should
write just the deep intake of breath as you pulled me in and
held me, soft pulse at the end of my fingers inside your
body and the flesh of sky fearless birdsong
at 9 a.m. yesterday in your house as we said good-bye.

SHORT HISTORY OF LOVE

Before the meadows of Dachau became Dachau
they were meadows. There was a small grove of tall pines
next to a flat stream with wide curves.
Painterly grasses full of variegated light.
Tall summery clouds. This is the painting your mother
brought over from Wurzburg. Before the Nazis took the house.
Some furniture. This painting and the painting
of the woman with her head bowed. She is naked.
You showed me where the soldiers took an ax to it.
The painting has been repaired.
You can hardly see that anything happened.
Wurzburg your mother says was a picture book town.
Your father's parents left behind in Berlin.
No money to get them out.
Which camp were they sent to?
What year were they killed?
My father was one of the first GIs into Orduff.
He wrote home to my mother:
How does anyone return from this?
I have seen things no one should ever see.
When I tell you I'm sad, you tell me: *Change the channel.*
When I tell you I miss you, you tell me: *Get busy.*
There was a time before and a time before
and there's a painting to prove it.
And your paintings on the walls too. Vermont
landscapes.   Good, solid meadows. Clouds.
The light expanding and coming toward us all.
It's a lot to compete with.

BETWEEN A POEM AND A SENTENCE

You've got no bra on and no underwear
you're on the couch of your new in-laws so to speak
and they tell you they don't get poetry

that dark machine clicking beneath you
that kooky singing all those weird caterwaulers
and you naked under your clothes you've

just come in from swimming in their blue pool
surrounded by beds of flowers
and you the only one swimming side to smooth side

and up beneath the zinnias the magenta daisies
tell me the difference between a good sentence and a poem
he says and what the hell do you know

but to talk about their daughter's latest painting the one
with the nude that seems to be lifting out of a tight
house the way you feel when she has her hand inside you

and she's taking you in your skin at the end of her tongue
heaving you up over the other houses that great salt dark
of your body leaving the bed altogether you're on the edge

of your seat now aware of your cool loose breasts inside
your shirt and making sure to keep the legs together
naked beneath your shorts and starting to lecture now

about poetry and what makes a poem a poem and a sentence
a sentence and the mother and father are nodding but then
you can tell you've gone too far and it's all you can think about

later driving home to your own home down the highway the black
of the night larger than the lights on the road and the darkness
going up from the ground and you know it's not stopping it just goes

THE HOUSEPAINTER BEFORE ME

A month painting the house and the cat getting thinner as we painted.
The story Mickey told as we laid the extension ladder on the slant
of the roof, pinned the ends of it into the lawn, then with bungee-cords
secured a step ladder to the top because the extension wasn't quite long enough
to get the unpainted boards the housepainter before me had left unpainted
the 8 years he'd lived here. He still appears on the road dropping cans of empty
Bud as he drives which is why I surmise his marriage ended and he had to sell
the house he built. Ancient crushed cans rise from behind the shed
like shards of glass suddenly shining in the skin after a car accident.
We were trying to figure out how to anchor the person on the ladder
so she wouldn't get catapulted off and sent Mickey to the top but did not tie
        her to the chimney
as in the story she told us about the man afraid of falling from his pitched
roof that was leaking in bad storms so he looped a rope around the chimney,
tied the end of the rope to the bumper of his car and the other end around his
        waist
but his wife forgot and started to drive to town. Mick doesn't know
how far the wife got before noticing husband screaming at the end of rope
as she was hauling him up the roof toward the chimney because
it wasn't her story to begin with, it was her Grandmother Blanche
told it about a month before she died and a month after Mick and I
stopped being lovers; she must've been trying to cheer granddaughter up
and then she was gone, and last week the cat who had been getting
thinner all month, died. I sat beside him while my lover called
from the kitchen wanting to know where to put the empty milk bottle
and an ad on TV was promising the Wild Animal Kingdom
for just 269 a month—*All of Nature at Your command*—rivers pouring
into the front seat, dolphins leaping, and the driver in his kayak inside the car.

The cat was in the living room on a soft bed dying, his breath short
and shallow, heartbeat barely discernible. When the fleas appeared
on the outside of his fur, I knew then he was really dead, the body no longer
viable and the fleas looking to go somewhere else, yet I had no idea
how still the house would feel after I wrapped him in a blanket
and buried him in the back yard, my lover gone home and Mickey with her
new girlfriend. Who knows where that man with the rope around his waist
tied to the bumper of the car looped around the chimney, went,
what his name is, or even where the story took place, Blanche buried
in upstate New York and it's all the ballast we get laughing at the top
of the ladder we should never have climbed in the first place;
nothing we did that day was safe.

SMACK THE HAM

Doors are clothing. Doors are clothing.
Stand clear of the door.
It's a beautiful, red brick house
Real muslin curtains.
Stand clear of the door.
Jane is the cook but she never cooks.
Two red lobsters, a ham, a fish,
some pudding. Some pears.
All of it extremely beautiful.
The food won't come off the plates.
A lovely dinner on the table.
Knives. Forks. Take your knife to the ham
and it won't cut. The ham breaks the knife.
Chop at the ham with your fork.
With the tongs. Then with the shovel.
It rolls off the table.
The ham flies into pieces.
It's a welter of forms.
The fish is glued to the dish.
The peas are plaster.
The pudding is plaster.
There's no end to your rage
and disappointment. Break up
the pudding. The lobsters.
Throw the fish in the fire.
The fire doesn't burn.
Chimney has no soot.
Don't go about in full daylight.

Doors are clothing.
Stand clear of the door.
Stand clear of the door.

after Beatrix Potter: *The Tale of Two Bad Mice*
and the shuttle bus, Washington National

MAYBE THE PORK CHOPS WERE DRY

Easier to have been the girl standing at the sink
singing *He's got the whole world in his hands*
and Daddy clapping at the end of the song;
easier to have been the butterball, the one who

laid her face in the butter, left shiny marks
everywhere she went; easier to have been the horse
the girl rode and the trail the horse trotted on;
easier to not have been the one who fell in love

with the girls carrying razor blades and tiny slits
up and down their arms then married a man
with bad teeth and had two children, and *just as easy*
her mother always said *to fall in love with a rich man*

as a poor man but she wasn't in love and the man
had no money and she could have stayed
with the woman she fell in love with who loved her
but she fell in love with another woman

who didn't and easy to talk about Father
who was so easy to hate because he was something
you could locate but now he's not so easy
because he's getting smaller and Mother

tells him stand up straight; easier to talk about them,
Father turning his dish upside down on the table
because the food was not hot, Mother standing
at the stove with her lip zipped and the children

afraid to move though the food seemed hot enough
to them but maybe the pork chops were dry.
It's that lesson about marriage
and the door you don't walk out of.

She could talk about them all day, Grandmother
in her chair in the rest home tilting forward saying
she wants to die; she's got no feet on the ground at all
as if one more adjustment of the chair and off she'd go.

THE WIND LIKE TRAFFIC

Trees tonight rocking by their roots, the wind like traffic
over the house.   Ecstatic. Cold. Clear.
You'd think that the broken limbs dangling
from the oak, twisting in the wind, ripped bark
holding it, you'd think the limb would
fly off in the wind, but the filaments hold
and it swings
as the forest rocks on its stems
and the wind takes whatever warmth there was in the air
off with it. You would think the house
might sail, the forest founder.
There are only the stars in the sky,
then the black around each star.
The moon is not out.
The moon is not nudging at each window
is not trying to get into the house
light up the rooms where I last saw you.

A Spoilt, Exquisite Air, Or Why I Won't Be Here When You Get Here

For in almost every artist nature is inborn a wanton and treacherous
proneness to side with the beauty that breaks hearts.

Death in Venice, Thomas Mann

I would like to say it was the marble floors.
That the town was too tidy. Too many tourists.
That a marriage ended in this flat.
That my eyes have gotten worse.
I waited at these windows, listened
to the footsteps on the stones outside.
Heard the talkers in their intimacy walking.
It could have been the forked wall with its finned top.
The four pigeons on the adjacent roof.
Maybe it was the mirrors in the house,
floor to ceiling. Wall to wall in the bedroom.
I saw us in the mirrors together
but then I didn't. I'd like to say
it's the neighbors' cool gaze,
or the hierarchy of boats on the green lagoon.
It was because there were so many boats.
Because of the landlord's affairs with tourists.
The wife he no longer lives with.
The spoons she counted before I moved in.
The forks in the drawer, and the spatula
that's about to break. Maybe the landlord
took a lover in this flat. In front of the mirror.
I imagined myself with you and then unimagined us.

Maybe the boat came and I got on it
because it was there. I waited for you in this city
and then I didn't. I will be gone when you get here.
Maybe I wanted from you what no one
should want from anyone. I lay in that bed
night after night and then I got up and left.
Maybe I made you up.
Perhaps the marble floors were too much.
I cried about you and then I didn't.
I won't be here when you arrive.
I would like to say I forgave you for what happened,
but it looks like I didn't.
I waited and then I wasn't waiting any longer.
Something broke and I went forward with it broken.
Yesterday, riding the boat back from Lido,
I imagined you tasting the salt on my skin,
and then I didn't.

THE LEISURE ACTIVITY OF COUPLES

It must be some kind of leisure activity.
Women grooming their men in public, leaning in
on a blemish. They do it on the beach.
In the store. On the bus. She grooms him
and he stays still under her hands.
On vacation without you, I have been studying couples.
How they identify themselves. Matched sets almost,
color coded. A united front.
Even the Italian couple brand new on the beach,
and the two of them not talking. A unit.
His face was turned toward her but not looking at her.
Neither standing or sitting, she was scrawling something fierce
on a scrap of paper. I had to get up and move.
Didn't want them between me and the water.
I recognized the activity. Both looking for that word
that's going to make the other one finally get it.
I didn't want to be reminded of it—
nor your heat on top of me
or the smell of your skin in this place.
How do people do it year after year?
Looks like harmony. Looks like you know where you are;
you're there and you like it.
At home last week walking through the January dark,
I stood under the smooth black stone of the sky
outside the house of the man whose wife of 50 years had just died.
I saw the blue light of the TV and heard that muffled voice
talking inside the light, and all the rest of the house
blank and dark.   Who would invite that kind of absence?

IV

Whatever it is that pulls the pin, that hurls you past the boundaries of your own life into a brief and total beauty, even for a moment, it is enough.

Jeanette Winterson

The Monument on Top of It

You cannot solder an Abyss/With Air

Dickinson #546

Last night over the subway grate at 1 a.m., I looked down and saw
there was no bottom to the hole and I was walking over it.

It is what I dreamed about when I was a girl,
a door in the floor of the world and it's open.

In my picture of marriage there's someone standing
before that door. You and that person speak the same language.

There's a pair of eyes looking back at you.
Even the bad marriage. Someone has a claim on you, knows your name

and wants to know just where you think you might be falling to.
In my fantasy, there's a strangeness that gets avoided.

This morning the man at the sink in the hallway
wanting to instruct me in French about how to use the bathroom light.

Wants me to leave the seat up. Would rather not see me
nor I him when I walk down the hall to the toilet that stinks.

Neither of us wants the other there.
We are strangers and don't know each other's name and don't want to.

They build monuments on it. Churches with huge domes.
Something heavy over the top of it.

There's the door and you are walking toward it so eagerly.
It's open and there's no one to see you step through.

You go through it because you can and the world's out there you say.
You can go out and fall as far as you want.

RED BOAT

Don't mistake the beached red boat for a body though it lies on the shore.
Though there's a place it could be rowed from. Ribs. A backbone. Gunnels.

It could float and you could row it. You could drift in it. Water would carry it
and you would go somewhere. It's seaworthy but the blue sky is not a face.

This is your body inside the boat. Lie down at the bottom. The boat holds you.
Contains you flat out of the wind, but you are not held by the boat. By the sky.

The sky won't take you though it fills your mouth. Your lungs. It does not love you.
The sunlight is good on your face like a hand. Make no mistakes though. You are in

a red boat beneath a blue sky listening to the sea. Crack of surf on the breakwater.
The air moving across your skin is not breath. The red boat is not a woman

on top of you or a woman beneath you. Is not a bed. Is not a trick doll either,
one of those dolls with the woman inside the woman

inside the woman smaller and smaller. You are not inside anything that has a top on it.
There is no lid, and you are not the little nub at the center.

Remember how it was as a child. The bright red doll on top of the piano.
How disappointing it was to come to the little woman at the center. The smallest doll.

She couldn't be opened up and there was no other little doll inside her.
Just a nub with a smile.

SHORT HISTORY OF SLEEP

In the dormitory with 15 other sleepers, she sat up and saw the breath
of all those women dreaming seemed to make a certain kind of light.
You could get up and walk around and see where you were going.
The air warm with the breathing and the women talking in their dreams.
It was a room full of sleep. It was like a fort. Alone in her house tonight
she thinks of the light in that room and the sound of those women breathing.
The comfort she found there. When she was a girl riding her horse home
in the dark toward the lights of the barn and the cows in their stanchions,
how could she have known then how quiet the world was sometimes going to be?
Her fingers cold in the dark but warm on the horse's hide.
The immense lungs of the horse beneath her on four hooves.
How wide the horse was. Big to wrap her legs around.
The horse carrying her back to the barn, to the breath of the cows in their stanchions.
That incubator. The warm wet of it and the lights always on somewhere in the barn.
Sometimes the radio playing softly to keep the herd company.
How was she to know that everything after this would be small?
What happens when the only breath in the house night after night is your own?
It astonishes her how much light you need the body to make by itself.
You lie there in the night and you breathe and you try to make the dark move.
We have to forgive ourselves that failure.
Last night the old man coming up the street drunk at 2:30 am.
How long it took him to get over the footbridge, around the corner
and up the alley. Alone, he was fighting with himself all the way up the street.
His voice echoed inside the stone walls. The argument like a dog
at the end of his body pulling.

THE SHARP AND BITTER IRRITANT OF KNOWLEDGE

Although I have not seen them touch, I know the two men down the beach from me
are lovers. They have been lying in the sun next to the abandoned sailboat and now
they are putting on their outer clothes, and one has stood up abruptly.
It is the abruptness of sexual love. Of marriage. He has picked up the mast of the boat
and thrust it down on the ground. Something has gone too far. Whatever he said
disappeared into the beach sand emptied of the man and woman who had been kissing
in front of us all and the dog named Laslo and the boy who ran after Laslo calling
his name. The man standing up is being emphatic about something. I recognize it—
that sudden despair because of that fierce thing lovers want from each other.
Because they give what it hurts to want and ask you not to want it. You want it and then
you make sure you don't. The man in his fury starts off toward the cabanas,
each blue and white house, 150 of them with its tiny porch, its blue trim, identical.
The official season is over. The ones who sat and played chess in front of the cabanas
are gone. The guilty man in the orange shorts begins to follow his lover first one way
then the other ten yards behind. Finally it looks like they're side by side
and the one man's hands have become quiet, no longer looking like they need
to hit someone, need to remove something from the body . How lovers promise
something with the skin that can't be erased after they're gone. The mouth. The lips.
Those exacting fingers. Ease the heart open. Invite you to step from your body.
Know exactly how to help you forget yourself, and then there you are
on a public beach waving your arms not even caring if somebody's watching.
I'm watching and doing what I can to forget you.

title from Thomas Mann: Death in Venice

ELEGY

Gold tree full of blackbirds shaking in a red sky at 6:15 pm.—
The beauty this world makes
as it goes. And the crickets

elegiac. Even the trees tick. Acorns ripping leaves
as they fall. Sound like scissors dropping.
Who could forget, the number of cells are finite,

and the place of memory simply a skull?
The frogs have climbed to the tops of trees to catch
the sun as it goes down. They turn toward the light

spread their silk throats and the trees vibrate with sound.
Something is taking mercy on us as it goes.
Consoling us for the disappearance.

For what will be taken back.
This morning I held the cat to my chest.
He is bone and hair who went with me

17 years, 12 houses. Through the two children
growing up. His heartbeat dim
beneath my finger. It is October. The songbirds have gone south

and the trees are brilliant with absence.
Never such a year for color people say, and the acorns
and apples abundant. Soon we will be able to count the sounds

that rise to the surface.
Be comforted by distillation. By what stands still,
and then, how one thing moves through it.

SHORT HISTORY OF GRAVITY

The faith in the trees standing around the house
should be reasonable. The massive trunks will stay up.
The limbs sticking into the light will stay lit.
Will not try to bury themselves on the forest floor.
That the light they grow upwards to reach will go on
convincing them upward. The forest won't fall on us.
And the spangled leaves pulling in the sunlight.
The pretty trees swaying in the wind. It's bucolic.
The wind high-pitched and the white pines full of it.
The way they bend both ways and come back and come back.
How to understand what keeps them standing?
That circle of wood that goes up and tapers to a point.
And all around us evidence of breakage.
You see them lying across the trail where you walked
but didn't happen to be walking the day the tree fell.
See the branches driven into the ground.
The collapse like a body going down without arms.
The dead pine standing behind the house.
It's bigger and rounder and taller and older.
If it were to fall onto the house, the house would break.
It's like any kind of faith.
And the sway, the rub of trunk on limb,
the sound almost of sex beginning.
Something being winched in the woods,
and the heavy, dark, pretty trees swaying in the moonlight.
There's the beauty of the world and you're in it.

NOBODY MOVE

The drunk staggering through the intersection of Rte. 5 and Main
made us all wonder if we were stopping in the right place.
Do you go right around an island, or do you do a loop
and come back the other side?
Which of us was supposed to stop, or should we all
just stand still in the heat, nobody move?
Who was it holding his hand before he came like water
into the intersection, bottle bobbing in his left hind
pocket? Who was it trying to talk some sense into him,
Come on, get in the car, you're being ridiculous, but gave up
and drove away? At first I thought they were lovers,
two men holding hands on a street corner in Greenfield.
What can you do with a drunk? Even the heat on his head,
that brightness on his hands shimmering as he stepped
toward an oncoming car the driver not sure to go left or go
right but certainly to stop if he had the green light at all.
I thought of that game with the rolling ball and the board
you wobble just to keep the ball from falling into the hole.
You have to keep tilting the surface. I waited for him to get
to the other side, thought about his friend driving away.
That particular practice. How we have to perfect it sometimes—
shut the door. Walk down the walk. Maybe it's the last time
you'll see that person. How can we not call each other by the names
of the ones we've lost? A certain red shirt. A gesture.
They come toward us like rain on a hot day.
You can smell the rain coming from the next town over.
Necessary, but we don't want it. The flowers dry, and the grass
waving heavy headed by the side of the road.
That brittle walk in the heat.

PLENITUDE

What slept in the crevice of the house has come awake in the October sun.
There's ladybugs on every window pane. Such a good omen my friend says
leaving town. A symbol of good karma. Everything buzzing. Wings shining
in the sunlight all over the door, the side of the barn. They fly in with us.
A beetle for each lid. Good luck looks like a plague. Then the black dog
with his face full of quills. A white beard. The happiness he had in the woods.
The discovery. The fat, slow-moving mammal, and the lair uncovered.
Something he could get his face on. In the abundant wood. Sunlight in every eye.
Wind like a vehicle in each leaf. Sky and cloud all over us. The green field,
the flock of goats, and the clicking trees. There's enough in town for everyone.
Down the street the neighbor has her vacuum out. She's sucking them up the tube.
Five ladybugs per inch of glass. This plenitude. When it's dark they'll drop
from the glass to the floor. The ladybugs will lay belly up until morning.
If you step on them there's a crackling noise. When winter comes they'll freeze
and be gone. There will be that steady tucking away of everything that moves.
Stick it all back into the hole in the wall. In the tree. In the ground out of which it
     climbed
to quill the dog who ran after the goats who ran soundlessly across the road
down the field to the barn who were greeted by their own dog who snarled
and tore into the intruder who ignored the woman begging him to come back.
He couldn't hear a thing. There was too much wind. The grass was so green
it blinded him. There were too many goats jumping in front of him.
Too much dog trying to tear out his throat. There's blood to be had. The great
snarl and snap of it all, this weird abundance— and the woman at the end
of the drive shouting into the wind *come back come back come back!*

The Resistance to Melancholy

Dog is like a barely built building falling as he walks down the stairs.
If a building could walk. Had fur and claws. Could drink out of toilets.
Dog sniffs at your face with his wet beard. He's pushing at the door.
He's the same pet everywhere you go. The wild at the end of the leash.
The pair of jaws, snapping, lunging at passing dogs. You can barely contain
him. The family coming towards you cower when the dog lunges and you say
bad dog.   There's that not so secret combination again. Embarrassment
and thrill. *He won't bite* you call out. You have to pull hard on the leash,
lean your whole weight against it, his white teeth snapping. In the car
on the way home, he lays his face in your lap and you forgive him.
He sees how easy people are, a little bit of fleshy contact,
some warm breath in the face. When he gets home, he gets loose.
Runs to the street, to the goats. You try to make him mind.
You go running after him waving your treat yelling, *Bad Dog. Sit Down.*
Come Back. Leash behind your back, a little bit of bacon in your fingers,
you're just a cartoon character with a round bubble at your lips.
Go ahead shout. Wave the bacon in the air. The goats are terrified.
Milk leaks from their teats. They leave a trail of white across the green field.
Why let your goats loose if you don't want them chased you'd like to know.
You're on the edge of tears, but then there you are again, you're almost
clapping for that bad dog. Who could resist that kind of glee? How neatly
he manages the melancholic goats, a little snap at the heels, and off they go.

GOING OUT OF BUSINESS

You haven't seen her for four months and then there she is on the other side
of the street in the coat you once urged her not to wear and a cap pulled down

deep on her head and she looks smaller than you remember.
She's walking quickly and doesn't see you staring at her, and you consider

calling to her from your side of Main Street, across traffic and the slush
of a new storm, but it would have to be a loud yell, a big bellow.

She's in front of a store *Going out of business*, it says in giant red letters
across the glass front: *Final Clearance, Everything Must Go.* She opens the door,

walks into the store never seeing you across the street with the pocket of air
cupped in your lungs because you were getting ready to yell but remembered

how feeble your scream really is nothing that would draw a crowd or stop someone
across the street, something not quite big enough in the larynx or a little door closed

between the diaphragm and the voice box. How good it is sometimes at the movies
to hear somebody really scream that un-stopped alarm rising from the body

straight up from the bottom of the belly rattling tongue, teeth, lips, that blast of sound
flooding the theater. You watched her disappear through that door

and didn't go after her. There you are on the street with that gulp of sound
you swallowed, traffic moving slowly in the new snow on Main Street, but steady.

After the Cows Go

That you can die, and die, and live again.
A man sings in the empty market at 5:30 a.m.
about what he can't have.
And Christ in his graphic losses.
Lost knees, hands, feet.
In each church you see his broken skin.
That you saw a dog run over in the street
and you go on living.
You live. Juice of the mango
runs down your arms and you cannot contain
that sweet in your mouth.
There's a feast in front of you
and a child with broken skin
begging at your elbow.
You give money.
You will go on eating.
That you lie in the arms of your lover
and the next morning pound the bed
with your fist, say you don't want
to see her again. Something dies,
but then you come back.
I'm sorry, you say, whisper in her ear,
forgive me. How many times
do you get to go under, and come up?
Skin on the ground behind you
like a coat you might drop
from your shoulders.
Empty cow hide on the floor

of the slaughterhouse.
As if the cows had simply
decided on something else
and moved on.
Corral at the center and the four cows
staring at the sky, smell blood—
hear the bellows of pigs behind them.
Unzip the hide. Lift from the house.
To die and die, and come back
in some other form, sail without skin
through the sound of bells
in a fine rain falling.